Don't Beat Your Children

Or

They'll Turn Out Like Me

By

BLUE

Copyrights ©2007 Derrick Wilson
TX-6-611-336

Library Of Congress Catalog Number

International Standard Book Number
ISBN 978-0-9712581-4-3
ISBN: 0-9712581-4-7

Published by
                 The Great Persuader Publishing
                        P.O. Box 1100
                      New York NY 10030

This book is a work of fiction. names, characters, places and incidents are either the product of the author's imagination or used fictitiously, and any resemblance to actual person, living or dead, events, or local is entirely coincidental.

Cover design and layout by Derrick Wilson
Printed In the United States of America

Photos on back cover - Chris Carr

You only live once

Therefore everything that you do
should be considered a big deal…

True Story

The only difference between Chicken and Beef
Is that it's hard to choke your Beef

Girl Power

In one pubic hair a women
has enough electricity
to jump start
New York City

Barista

A Poem for the Girl in the Harlem coffee shop

If you were the Coffee
Then I'll be the Biscotti

That's because you're Black and Hot

And I am Hard and a little Nutty...

Rough Diamonds...

A Poem for the Girl in the Brooklyn coffee shop... LOL

'I met this Diamond in Starbucks, by the name of Tiffany

I once asked her to pass the cream
but instead she gave me the finger

So I put It into my drink

and now it's even richer...

Pretty In Pink

*A Poem inspired by the Attractive Lady
on the A Train*

Pink was never a favorite color of mine
until I saw you in it...

Brooklyn Girl

A Poem inspired by the Attractive Lady
on The Brooklyn bound Q-train

She sat across from me with a vintage leather jacket on
She had her hair in cornrows and her jeans were rolled up like a
cowgirl...

Home girl had eyes like a six shooter
and I wanna tell her how good she looks
but I'm afraid she'll shoot me...

Sweet Tooth

A Poem inspired by the Attractive Lady
on The Brooklyn bound N-train

She had a face like a cake
and I wish that I was the baby
invited to her birthday party…

Lost

*A Poem inspired by the Attractive Lady
on the # 2 Train, when I needed directions*

Her Locks had me twisted
And once I stopped spinning

I found myself, trying to find my self...

Haiku

Love Is Sweet

"Love is sweet" said she
The echoes of her whispers
Vibrate in my heart

Haiku
Girls Gone Wild
*A poem inspired by the rowdy girls
on the B-Train*

Behaving like nuts
in order to have a ball

Wait 'till Dad finds out...

C P T

Slim goodie
give men Woodies
you remind me of a lollipop

You got legs like licorice sticks
and dimples like gums drops

Plus your smile that's so sweet
that it made me miss my stop...

Haiku

Spring Flower

She's my spring flower
and I'm losing altitude
Help, Mayday... May Day!

Daydreaming
In my sleep

I guess the only reason
that I never dream about you,
is because I stay up all night
just thinking about you...

Give this poem to that special someone...

Spare Time

A Poem inspired by the Attractive Lady
on The Manhattan bound J- train

If I had one wish,
I would beg for time and I'd take all that I could carry

I would fill my front pockets with hours

And my back pockets with days
And I would spend them only with you…

This one too!

Haiku

A Sweet Sticky Thang

*A Poem inspired by the Attractive Lady
on The Queens bound F- train*

Spinning from your kiss
My lips have your name on them
You sweet, sticky thang

Reflecting

Stars are actually the back of nails,
which prevents the sky from falling...

Telephone Love

*A Poem inspired by the Attractive Lady
on The Bronx Bound 4- Train*

Hold me
the way that u hold your cell phone...
Up to your ear
and close to your mouth...

Telephone Lust

A Poem inspired by the Attractive Lady
on The Manhattan bound D - Train

Put your cell phone on vibrate
Sit it on your lap,
And I'll call you when I'm coming...

Skin Deep 1

The only difference
between a Pretty Girl and a Ugly Girl is,

The ugly girl is a better cook...

Skin Deep 2

The Only difference
between a Pretty Girl and a Ugly Girl is,

The pretty girl has been screwed more...

Mi aime jou!

Your Voodoo has got to be a good thing

Now you have me under your spell
and I'm telling everybody
that I'm just crazy about you...

This lady once told me that my poems are dirty and I shouldn't read them aloud because she was offended. And then I told her, the two of the biggest urges that humans have are Food and Sex, which leads to obesity and unwanted pregnancies. And this is more prevalent in the ghetto's then anywhere else. And thats dirty too...

Talking Dirty

Being overweight in America is proof
that we do not reproduce by exercising
I am a product of my parent's
Their bed was not a bike

So, there is nothing dirty about sex-
However Poetry can be

Good poetry is sexy
but great Poetry is what made me…
Dirty

Book sense

Toting thick books along with her awesome looks
Man was she was stacked...
Hey!
Pretty lady why don't you just squeeze me into your thoughts
like a bookmark...

And this just might be the most important chapter of your life

Hypothetically

There we were lost
in the middle of the sea
Mother,
Me
and my wife to be…

And if this ship should sink,
whom should I save?

Haiku

Unlady Like

The girl that I like
is very unlady like
Yet, perfect for me

Unlady Like

THE DEEP VERSION

Girls only seem to check me out
whenever they see me with another girl

So I started hanging out with lesbians

And now we pick up chicks together...

All Jokes Aside

The ghetto is a funny place

Take it easy
and you might die
laughing...

Think Big!

Send your children to school
and teach'em how to steal
Legally,
because that's the American way...

A Vicious Cycle

1

Boys make babies then run

Women claim that all men are dogs
but they are the ones who raised them...

Haiku

A Vicious Cycle

2

A boy with no dad
grows up viewing life one way

How to be a trick…

Here's Your Present

Long braids touch tramp stamp
With bling-bling both earlobe
That's the new man - look

A Benign Hatred for men is when
a single mother gleams into her infant's eyes
Plays in his hair and then thinks aloud,

Dam son, you would make a cute girl!

A Quickie

If Poppa was a rolling stone
What are the chances
of him bumping into Mrs. Jones
And they producing me

The trick baby

Haiku

A Good Strap'n

Black children are bad?
However, if you beat them
they'll become good slaves…

Haiku

Word Son

How can a grown man
be taken seriously
when dressed like a boy?

Habla Mucho

*A Poem inspired by the loquacious Lady
on The # 5 Train*

The good thing
about learning
a new language
is...
You must think
before you speak

Haiku

Good Hair?

What's more important,
The texture of your child's hair
Or what's in their head?

Why do Baptist
send their babies
to Catholic School?

Life after death?

If you're dead
And you know that you are dead...

Then you are not dead

Haiku

Praying to the sky
For a spirit you can't see
Yet you call It, Him…

Haiku

Practical

Since God is so great
Why don't we just kill ourselves
to be by his side?

Haiku

Sexy Religion

I'm an atheist
Yet, whenever we make love
Then I doubt myself

Haiku

Gangster Rap 1

Italian gangsters
Dead and buried six feet deep
Live through rap music

Haiku

Gangster Rap 2

Italian gangsters
Some dead, buried six feet deep
Still live through Hip Hop

Starving Artist

I use to be a D.J. on an Ice cream Truck
Struggling to make ends meet
Surviving off of the food stuck in my teeth
and I spent my spare time begging for toothpicks

Haiku

Paper Chaser

Money grows on trees
I just can't afford the seeds
to plant in my yard…

Haiku

Credit Cards

If America
became a cash-less country
what would bums beg for?

Haiku

Good Taste

It's always the poor
Buying expensive clothing...
The rich get it free

Haiku

Back In The Days

You can guess my age
by the way I lace my shoes...

I'm from the old school

Haiku

Basket Cases

In the big apple
bad actors do a good job
of playing crazy...

Bulletproof

Bulletproof Corner Stores
never stop to take a breath
Catch a contact from the gun smoke

I come a place where the scent of
roach spray gets me homesick...

Blue-ku

Harlem University

I'm a proud student

of Harlem University
The school of hard Knocks

That is where I received my degree in Urban philosophy
under the tutelage of con-me and hustlers, fast talkers
and loose women with tight bodies...

Haiku

The School
Of Hard Knocks

Gurlz take whore practice
While the boyz dress for jail school

Welcome to the Hood

Neighborhood

Across the street from the Housing projects
there is a pet shop...

Now this is insane,
because you would think that after living so long
in a cramped up situation,
somebody might show some compassion
for a goldfish in a bowl with no where to go,
but in circles...

or a caged up Black Bird with a broken soul...

Haiku

Wassup Dawg?

Big Dawgs taking walks
Marking their territory
Better watch your step...

Haiku

Wassup Dog?

Neighbors walk their dogs
Leaving feces on sidewalks
Squish! Dam, Good luck stinks!

The Ghetto

Prayers travel through air
like clouds of smoke
Yet pollution,
gets all of the attention....

If life is a game,
Who's Playing?

And if we are a race,

Who's winning?

Haiku

Life

The world is fucked up
Yet we keep making babies
to live in this shit...

Blue-Ku

Spilt milk

On cold Harlem streets
Dopefiends fill baby bottles
with Hot milk from Starbucks

Haiku

Back Pain

Senior citizens
wearing shoes with Velcro straps...
Rheumatism hurts!

Haiku

Black People

We hold funerals
and family reunions

All in the same breath…

Haiku

She's Charlize Theron

African Americans
come in all flavors

Haiku

Black

Brown - Red- Yellow- White
African Americans
Come in all colors

Haiku

Friends and Family

Friends and Family
only call when they need me...
That's how they show love

Mad Churches
In Brooklyn

A poem inspired by the street politicians

Yo!
You can't argue with a stop sign...

Every Mind
Is A World

S treet corner politicians try to convert my thoughts by telling me, That there will come a time when we will all have the same mind.

One God
A grand family acting in unison for one agenda
And my reply was, "Yeah… That's called cloning."

Haiku
Golden Silence

Please don't ignore me...

Your silence beats my eardrums
It makes my blood stink

Haiku

Hot Grits

Love n Happiness?
She played me like the organ
From an Al Green hit

Summer time

was intended for women...

It's when they dress the best
It's when they wear less

It's when that summer breeze
be blowing through that linen dress
and it be giving me chills,
making me sneeze...

And she turned around and started blessing me!

Haiku

Forty -Seconded Street
was once like a Disco tech
where players Hustled

Haiku
Flashing

Gang bangers throw signs
As if, they are dumb and death

Dumb yes- but not Def...

EVOLUTION

Sweet Brown Sugar has always been considered a hot commodity and prior to my neighborhood being gentrified, you would have men from the suburbs risk their lives for a piece;

They would tiptoe through Ghetto like a thief in the night
Producing High yellow babies that could pass for white
Now them girls in the suburbs got Ghetto backsides
They like hip-Hop music and Usher, getting on the dance floor and dropping It like it's hot while speaking in Ebonics and talking 'bout "I hear that"
That's called evolution
It's those silly Negro's sitting on the stoop that thinks that it's their silly words that's gon' get them to second base not realizing that women call the shots...
Now, the only reason people glorify the "Ghetto" is because it gives it this commercial connotation
I'm say'n that there's a profit to be made off of poverty
Put a beat to my pain and I'm a slave to the dollar

And quiet as it's kept - the only reason that the emancipation proclamation ever went into effect is that the Founding Fathers knew that Black folks now had a firm grasp on the bible

They knew that we'd go from coast to coast to propagate our faith, by building store front churches and showing more compassion for something that happened more than two thousand years ago and show no concerns for the woes that plague The Hood today

If Black people stopped going to church for one week it would shake the foundation of this economical structure and that's when the Founding Fathers would use all of their resources to start building fences around the suburbs quicker than you could say, 'Good Ship Jesus'

But then again that's just a big IF cause cotton came to Harlem a long time ago

And while the Black men are still sitting on the stoop arguing about which girl has the fattest ass, every Ghetto in America is being gentrified...

A VICIOUS CYCLE
The Long version

D rugs have always flourished in my part of the town and we were always considered the seeds of a rotten apple with just enough sugar left at the bottom of our cereal bowls to keep us retarded, up until day one rolled around again.

But you know what it's like in the hood?

And society is always staring down my throat to make sure that I'm not about to steal sump'n

But when Black people 1st got to America, our credit was impeccable... it's the sharecropping that put us behind the 8 ball

And since that day, it's always gon' be some bullshit in the Hood and under it, covertly designed to keep these colored folks twisted

So society calls me the negative wire connected to the car battery...

Well, praying ain't gon' change that

In fact, somebody needs to tell these poverty pimps to stop acting like cheerleaders

They get holy only on Sunday while using the bible as leverage for tax incentives, good pussy, and a place to park

You can see the vanity all in their pose...

They want the world to come to an end so bad,
just so, they can have a good sermon the preceding Sunday
But they know that God is green America
Therefore Big Money is an illusion and the trickle down
effect was meant to fuck those living paycheck to paycheck while
steadily enforcing their slave mentality
So what's the point of wearing a band-aid if it's not gon' stop
my bleedin'
I'm heated,
My blood stinks and it feels as though the weight of 44 mil-
lion black folks is on my back
Man, hell can get cold
In fact it has the potential to freeze over everyday
It comes off like a glare from this ghetto bastard, the boy
who never knew that it was geometrical feasible for a man to stand
in front of the toilet, lift the seat and take a piss...
Until his mother's boyfriend taught'em how to do it
Now that's really Hood

All this time, he's been sitting on the toilet seat like a little
girl and that's only indicative of what takes place where men insist
on arguing with stop signs
And one day I'm gon' leave this place
but my money is funny
and that ain't funny...

Other books by The Great Persuader Include

Pretty Ugly, A Harlem Situation
· and

Corner Stores In The Middle Of The Block

for more information
visit the website

www.Poetryisalive.com

Myspace.com/Bradbathgate

Myspace.com/poetryisalive

The Great Persuader Publishing
P.O. BOX 1100
NEW YORK NY 10030